Our Reason to Hope

Our Reason to Hope

George R. Ross

RESOURCE *Publications* • Eugene, Oregon

OUR REASON TO HOPE

Resource Publications
An Imprint of Wipf and Stock Publishers
199 W. 8th Ave., Suite 3
Eugene, OR 97401
www.wipfandstock.com

ISBN 13: 978-1-60899-847-0

Manufactured in the U.S.A.

But in your hearts sanctify Christ as Lord. Always be ready to make your defense to anyone who demands from you an accounting for the hope that is in you; yet do it with gentleness and reverence. Keep your conscience clear, so that, when you are maligned, those who abuse you for your good conduct in Christ may be put to shame. (1 Pet 3:15–16)

Have you ever noticed how often the word spirituality is bantered about in people's conversations, especially if the topic of discussion is religion? "I am not a religious person," one individual will argue, "*but I am spiritual!* I don't go to church or anything like that, *but I am spiritual!* I do believe in a higher power, but this Jesus stuff is not for me. *But I am spiritual!*"

This reminds me of the story of an alcoholic who joined Alcoholics Anonymous to help him stop drinking. Others in the group indicated that he needed to place his faith in a higher power. So he proceeded to place his faith in a beautiful thirty-foot-high oak tree. Remarkably, he remained free of alcohol for nearly twenty-five years. But then one day an ice storm hit his tree and it was destroyed. Needless to say, so was the poor soul's sobriety. As he sat in the bar, drunk once again, he lamented the loss of his limited and finite "higher power" that served as the core of his spirituality.

The *Westminster Dictionary of Theological Terms* (1996, p. 268) defines spirituality as "the quality of being spiritual (pertaining to the spirit or nonmaterial)." Elaborating, the dictionary explains that "historically, varieties of spiritualities have emerged relating to different religious traditions. They take place through rituals and practices." Other writers point out (Miller and Thoresen, 1999, pp. 5–9) that "for at least as long as history has been recorded, humankind has assumed that reality is not limited to the material, sensory world"—that which we see, hear, touch, taste, and smell. For spiritual reality embraces the intangible, "be it belief in supreme being or order, life after physical death, an ultimate reality, or supernatural beings like angels or demons."

Spirituality often serves as an important source of strength and direction in people's lives. Whereas religion portrays our attempts to relate to that which is sacred or divine, spirituality, in contrast, embraces our subjective experiences, often involves "a highly personal and private matter, and usually focuses on intangible elements that provide vitality and meaning to life."

One writer, Ernest Kurtz, explains that spirituality helps "the alleviation of mental, emotional, and spiritual distress thought to be at least in part caused by a lack of an appropriate relationship with ultimate reality, most often signaled by and reflected in inappropriate relationships with other people or things." Kurtz emphasizes that "any spirituality is a lived theology, a posture that positions one within total reality," for spirituality embraces "sanity, sanctity, serenity, health, wholeness, and holiness." He concludes that spirituality is "an attitude, a posture of one's very being that allows seeing not different things but everything differently." Simply stated, spirituality is that "for which all persons strive." It is our guiding compass.

For me personally, spirituality becomes less complex and more tangible when I realize that it simply involves seeking out and confronting life's issues of ultimate concern. Spirituality emerges in our lives when we look for and struggle with the answers to such life questions as: What should I value in life? How should I conduct myself in my interactions and relationships with others? What kind of character do I want to develop? How do I deal with my own imperfections (or may I say my sins) and the imperfections (or may I say the sinful nature) of others? How do I cope with the assumingly finite nature of my life and that of those for whom I love and care? Or more succinctly asked, what constitutes life and what constitutes death?

How we answer these five questions often reflects our religious convictions and the impact they have had on our spiritual growth and development. In fact, we could conduct a comparative analysis of all the world religions based on how they addressed these five ultimate questions of concern. In so doing I have discovered, that for me, Christianity offers a more complete and the most satisfying response to these questions of ultimate concern.

Therefore, I invite you to join with me this morning as we examine together how a Christian response to these five questions of ultimate concern positively shapes and molds our spiritual growth and, more importantly, validates "our reason to hope." Join with me this morning, as we better prepare ourselves to share the good news of the gospel of Jesus Christ to an inquiring hurting world that is puzzled by our inner joy and often desperately seeks to obtain the hope that abides within us.

To ask what you value in life is a spiritual question. It aims directly at the heart. It addresses the issue as to how I should spend my time and money. It asks: toward what purpose or purposes should I direct my talent, energy, and resources? For example, when I conduct parenting workshops I ask the fathers in the class this question: "What do you value more, Sports Center or your children?" They resoundingly answer, our children! Then I ask them: "How much time each week do you spend watching Sports Center, and how much time do you spend with your children?" Their answer for Sports Center usually involves several hours and for the children, but a few minutes. Then I ask again: "What do you value more, Sports Center or your children?" When the fathers return the next week to the class, many are eager to tell me that they have made a change. One father explains: "You will be pleased to know, Dr. Ross, that I have made a change and have invited my children and my wife to watch Sports Center with me."

In our bible reading this morning, Peter writes: "*but in your hearts sanctify Christ as Lord.*" Another rendering of the passage reads: "*but in your hearts set aside Christ as Lord.*" Careful biblical study makes it clear that as Christians we are to first develop an ongoing relationship with Jesus. Jesus is to be our primary value. Jesus first! Then the meaning and purpose in life becomes clear. We are to glorify God as we serve others with an attitude of love, justice, and mercy. We are to project a beacon of light onto a world of darkness sharing the faith of our hope in the victory of Christ over darkness and death. For as the apostle Paul writes in Romans 11:36 through Romans 12:2:

> *For from him and through him and to him are all things. To him be the glory forever. Amen. I appeal to you therefore, brothers and sisters, by the mercies of God, to present your bodies as a living sacrifice, holy and acceptable to God, which is your spiritual worship. Do not be conformed to this world, but be transformed by the renewing of your minds, so that you may discern what is the will of God--what is good and acceptable and perfect.*

I ask you this morning, are you seeking the will of God in your life? Which is more important, Sports Center or your relationship with Christ? How much time do you devote to meditation, bible study, and prayer? Paul encourages us in Philippians to:

Rejoice in the Lord always; again I will say, Rejoice. Let your gentleness be known to everyone. The Lord is near. Do not worry about anything, but in everything by prayer and supplication with thanksgiving let your requests be made known to God. And the peace of God, which surpasses all understanding, will guard your hearts and your minds in Christ Jesus. Finally, beloved, whatever is true, whatever is honorable, whatever is just, whatever is pure, whatever is pleasing, whatever is commendable, if there is any excellence and if there is anything worthy of praise, think about these things. (Phil 4:4–8 NRSV)

How are we to interact with others? This too is a spiritual question? In our bible passage this morning, Peter explains that we are to share "our reason to hope" with gentleness and reverence. Our interactions with others present a sacred opportunity to share the abiding hope we have in Christ. Christ explains in Matthew 22:37–40 that we are to interact with others with love.

He said to him, "'You shall love the Lord your God with all your heart, and with all your soul, and with all your mind.' This is the greatest and first commandment. And a second is like it: 'You shall love your neighbor as yourself.' On these two commandments hang all the law and the prophets."

The apostle Paul elaborates the meaning of love in 1 Corinthians 13: 4–8:

Love is patient; love is kind; love is not envious or boastful or arrogant or rude. It does not insist on its own way; it is not irritable or resentful; it does not rejoice in wrongdoing, but rejoices in the truth. It bears all things, believes all things, hopes all things, endures all things. Love never ends. But as for prophecies, they will come to an end; as for tongues, they will cease; as for knowledge, it will come to an end.

So as followers of Jesus we are commanded to love one another. But if we take an honest inventory of ourselves, we often fall short of Paul's descriptors of love. And if we really were honest with ourselves we would have to honestly admit "we have loved but a few; that we have been quite indifferent to the many so long as none of them gave us trouble; and as for the remainder—well, we have really disliked or hated them." We will begin to experience real love for others when we start to realize "that all people, including ourselves, are to some extent emotionally ill as well as frequently wrong. (AA, p. 92)" Or as Paul explains it in Romans 3:10, *"there is no one who is righteous, not even one."*

What kind of character do I want to develop? Or now that I have decided to no longer be a character, what kind of virtues do I want to emulate? This too is a spiritual question. And the Bible, as with the first two spiritual questions, gives us some definitive answers. Turn with me to Galatians 5:22–23. *"By contrast, the fruit of the Spirit is love, joy, peace, patience, kindness, generosity, faithfulness, gentleness, and self-control. There is no law against such things.*" By contrast, the Bible encourages us to develop a character, a set of virtues that will offset our sinful nature as the indwelling power of the Holy Spirit transforms us from our iniquities into the image of Christ. Paul explains in Gal 5:19–21 that:

> *The acts of the sinful nature are obvious: sexual immorality, impurity and debauchery; idolatry and witchcraft; hatred, discord, jealousy, fits of rage, selfish ambition, dissensions, factions and envy; drunkenness, orgies, and the like. I warn you, as I did before, that those who live like this will not inherit the kingdom of God.*

But fortunately, he reminds us in Galatians 5:24–25 that "*those who belong to Christ Jesus have crucified the flesh with its passions and desires.*" Therefore, "*if we live by the Spirit, let us also be guided by the Spirit.*" Are you inviting the spirit of God to transform your life?

How to deal with our imperfections and the imperfections of others, that is, how do we cope with the sinful nature of both ourselves and others? This too is a spiritual question. Also the issues surrounding the limitation of our life, that is to say that we will eventually die physically, this too is a spiritual question. And quite profoundly, these two spiritual questions cut to the core of the Christian message and our reason to place our hope in Christ. Because Jesus made the ultimate sacrifice on the cross, and more importantly, because he rose again from the dead, because he has achieved victory over sin and death, we too can be *reconciled* in Christ, *transformed* in Christ, and *regenerated* in Christ.

Turn with me please to the book of Ephesians as we examine some key passages that illuminate the notions of reconciliation, transformation, and regeneration. Reconciliation involves bridging the gap between God and humanity due to our sinful nature. Christ's atoning blood reconciles us with God, spans the gap, and restores our relationship with God.

Paul reminds us of our condition before salvation in Eph 2:12. He reminds us of our condition without Christ. "Remember that you were at that time without Christ, being aliens from the commonwealth of Israel, and strangers to the covenants of promise, having no hope and without God in the world."

But Paul in Ephesians 2:13–16 explains: "We have been reconciled so that we now can be transformed into the image of Christ." Paul describes this transformation in Ephesians 4:17–25:

> *Now this I affirm and insist on in the Lord: you must no longer live as the Gentiles live, in the futility of their minds. They are darkened in their understanding, alienated from the life of God because of their ignorance and hardness of heart. They have lost all sensitivity and have abandoned themselves to licentiousness, greedy to practice every kind of impurity. That is not the way you learned Christ! For surely you have heard about him and were taught in him, as truth is in Jesus. You were taught to put away your former way of life, your old self, corrupt and deluded by its lusts, and to be renewed in the spirit of your minds, and to clothe yourselves with the new self, created according to the likeness of God in true righteousness and holiness So then, putting away falsehood, let all of us speak the truth to our neighbors, for we are members of one another. But now in Christ Jesus you who once were far off have been brought near by the blood of Christ. For he is our peace; in his flesh he has made both groups into one and has broken down the dividing wall, that is, the hostility between us. He has abolished the law with its commandments and ordinances, that he might create in himself one new humanity in place of the two, thus making peace, and might reconcile both groups to God in one body through the cross, thus putting to death that hostility through it.*

In this passage we have learned that we have been reconciled and transformed in Christ. But we are also regenerated in Christ.

A new life is implanted in us. The disposition of our soul is made holy. Paul explains the process in Ephesians 2:1–5

> *You were dead through the trespasses and sins in which you once lived, following the course of this world, following the ruler of the power of the air, the spirit that is now at work among those who are disobedient All of us once lived among them in the passions of our flesh, following the desires of flesh and senses, and we were by nature children of wrath, like everyone else. But God, who is rich in mercy, out of the great love with which he loved us even when we were dead through our trespasses, made us alive together with Christ—by grace you have been saved.*

This process of being *alive together with Christ* includes receiving his righteousness, being forgiven, being joint heirs with Christ, and being fully accepted by God. In Christ we have eternal security, that in Christ we come to be complete human beings.

Reconciled in Christ, *transformed* in Christ, and *regenerated* in Christ; I don't know about you, but I have not found a more complete package. In Christ, my life has purpose and meaning. In Christ I am able to love both my friends and my enemies. In Christ, I can develop a character worth emulating, a disposition that will bring hope to those who despair. In Christ, I can learn how to forgive others and myself and rest assured that I will spend eternity with God.

When we examine the Greek word translated as hope in the bible, we learn that it is also defined as an *expectation that we can look forward to with confidence, something in which we can ground our faith*. This is why I have set aside Christ in my life as both my Savior and Lord. In so doing, I now have a reason for hope, no longer fearing death, being alive together with Christ. If you have not yet made this decision, proclaiming Christ as Savior and Lord in your life, I encourage you to do so today, so you too may have a reason to hope.

References

AA (1991). Twelve steps and twelve traditions. New York: Alcoholics Anonymous.

Kurtz, E. (1999). The historical context. In W. R. Miller's (Ed.) Integrating spirituality into treatment. Washington, DC: American Psychological Association.

D. K. (1996). Westminster dictionary of theological terms. Louisville, KY: Westminster John Knox.

Miller, W. R. & Thoresen, C. E. (1999). Spirituality and health. In W. R. Miller's (Ed.) Integrating spirituality into treatment. Washington, DC: American Psychological Association.

The five questions of ultimate concern

1. What should I value in life?
2. How should I conduct myself in my interactions and relationships with others?
3. What kind of character do I want to develop?
4. How do I deal with my own imperfections (or may I say my sins) and the imperfections (or may I say the sinful nature) of others?
5. How do I cope with the assumingly finite nature of my life and that of those for whom I love and care? What constitutes life and what constitutes death?

For More Information Contact
George R. Ross, PhD; MDiv
60 Summertree Court
Nicholasville, Kentucky 40356
Telephone (859) 223-5126
e-mail 53049grr@insightbb.com
web page Georgerross.com